First Steps to MANAGING STRESS

Lynette Miller

AXIOM

ISBN: 1 86476 026 5

Axiom
Australia

The photographic images used in this book were obtained from IMSI's MasterClips Collection, 75 Rowland Way, Novato, CA 94945, USA.

Cartoons by
Stephen Emerson

Contents

page

Managing Stress

Managing Stress

This book is designed to give quick and easy access to information on stress and stress reducing strategies.

You can read through or just open to any page to find simple ways and 'spot' styles for coping.

Knowing what to do is helpful, but **doing it** is the only way to deal with stress.

Stress Happens!

Stress happens to everyone - male or female, young or mature - everyday.

Managing Stress

Stress can be defined as 'an arousal response to a person, an event or an object', so realising how many times we react each day, we can see that stress is experienced constantly.

There are two possible reactions:

- A happy and pleasurable reaction to positive things e.g. being praised.
- A fearful or distressing reaction to negative things e.g. being criticised.

There are also three different intensities of reactions:

- An immediate response which subsides as quickly as it starts.
- The second is a sustained burst, taking time to ease.
- The third, a response which continues for days, weeks and sometimes longer, heightening and reducing in intensity, **but maintained**.

Dealing With These Responses

- The first stress response will usually be dealt by mind and body. Calming, then returning to a balanced state called homeostasis.

- The second response needs to be dealt with to avoid prolonging the stress. Using simple 'spot' strategies will assist in again achieving the balance.

- The third reaction is the potentially destructive 'strain response' which requires considered strategies encompassing:
  - relaxation
  - recreation
  - rest

in order to restore both the body and the quality of life.

Using the 'spot' strategies as often as possible will also assist in stress reduction.

Note:

The main reason for stress strategies is to reduce response as quickly as possible, thereby restoring the balanced state of mind and body.

Stress For Best

The attitude 'more is better' keeps us focused on physical aspects of **accumulation** and **approval**.

You need not stop external pursuits to be at peace. However, you do need to make choices about what you are doing which is **life-enhancing**, and what you are doing which is **life-destroying**.

The following beliefs will raise stress levels and should be questioned:

- I must be busy to be fulfiled
- I must make more money to be secure
- I must be promoted to prove my worth
- I must have the latest and the best to be content
- I must do everything for everybody to be valued.

On the surface the needs to feel fulfiled, secure, worthy, content and valued are positive, but often the way we go about bringing these attributes into our lives can be negative, and possibly destructive.

Continually pursuing a more-is-better, external, exhausting lifestyle is often a way of not dealing with an empty, dissatisfied internal self.

Managing Stress

Attitude is all when dealing with this situation.

"But what if ... I'm not busy, don't get rich, am not promoted, own the latest or continually provide? What will my future be, how will I cope?"

Realistically "What is .... ?"

What is happening to you and your life while you are busy all the time accumulating, promoting yourself, acquiring and providing?

"What if ..." is a future focus,

"What is ...." is a present aspect.

Remember the future is not yet formed, the present is what will form it.

So **simplify** by:

- changing situations
- discarding objects
- avoiding negative people
- eliminating thoughts that are not positive, constructive and for your health and benefit.

Simplify to satisfy

Positive Pleasures

Small and simple strategies to bring pleasure to your life.

- Have a single flower in every room
- Put pictures you enjoy where you can see them constantly - in a drawer at work, on your desk, on the backs of doors, in your purse or wallet
- Have an object in view that reminds you of a good experience - a stone, a shell, etc
- Use oil burners to create an uplifting atmosphere
- Float flowers and leaves in a bowl of water - by the front door, on a table, etc
- Open wide the curtains to let in natural light
- Have a cassette of your favourite music playing in the car instead of listening to a depressing news report
- Put candles around the room, light them and sit down in the soft glow to relax
- Place crystals in spots where you are able to appreciate their beautiful qualities
- Hang wind chimes inside or outside your home

Choice and Price Paying

A great deal of our stress response comes about through **feelings of powerlessness**, and thoughts about **lack of control** over people, situations or ourselves.

Many people **believe** they are trapped and have no choices.

Essentially - you always have choices.

The dictionary defines choice as 'the determination of the mind in preferring one thing to another'. Although many times the options are not what you want, you presume to believe there are none, therefore, no change can be made.

When you are prepared to examine the choices to assist you in making a balanced judgement you can work with a strategy called **price paying**.

Choice and Price Paying

In every situation you will have a price to pay.

An example: if you are in a harmful relationship your options are to stay or leave.

If you stay, you will pay a price which may include unhappiness and lack of love.

If you leave, the price you pay may include feelings of failure and concerns for the future.

But by realistically (not catastrophically) working out the price you **could** pay and you are **prepared** to pay, you will be able to make a choice, which will give you back a feeling of control.

Note:

- **Think the situation through**
- **Consider the price you will be paying**
- **Choose your path of action**
- **Do it!**

Water

Being apprehensive or anxious will cause our bodies to produce stress chemicals. An increased intake of water is essential during these occasions.

Water

Hormones are released into your body, allowing you to function, e.g. adrenaline so you can fight and cortisol so you can flee. When we are continually anxious, drinking water will assist in flushing the excess hormones from the body.

Drink

one to two litres of water daily. Use small glasses and sip frequently rather than try to consume large quantities at one time.

Soak

in warm baths filled with bubbles or oils. Use candles and music to create a totally relaxing and enjoyable experience.

Shower

to feel warm water covering the whole surface of the body, cleansing and refreshing the skin.

After a shower or bath you can pat yourself dry with a soft fluffy towel to relax, wrap yourself in a large towelling robe and lay down to rest, or rub your skin vigorously with a dry wash cloth to improve circulation.

Creeks, Ponds, Fountains and the Ocean

are very calming. Have a favourite spot near water and plan some time, even if only a short period, to refresh yourself.

Enlightenment

To become 'enlightened' is a popular word in modern times, although few people understand the term.

The religious/spiritual aspect is to gain an awareness of Higher Consciousness. However, a more tangible aspect in terms of stress reduction is the level of the physical/mental attitude to enlightenment.

In a state of tension...we depress:

- our thoughts
- our body
- our feelings
- our lives.

Enlightenment

Release negative feelings

Our thoughts often depress us when thinking:

- "What's the use?"
- "It's all too hard"
- "Life's such a struggle"
- "I can't handle it" (the person, the situation, myself).

Depression causes our head to drop forward, our body to slouch, our neck and shoulders tighten and our eyes look down. A sense of apathy and numbness is felt.

We focus on negative thoughts to proceed with daily trials. It is as if we are carrying a large boulder of worries, fears and hurts.

The word anxiety is derived from the Latin 'to narrow' and it is easy to identify with, particularly when our lives have such a narrow perspective. It becomes difficult, if not seemingly impossible, to see anything positive in life.

Now For The Positives

Firstly, adjust your physical appearance:

- Lift your head so it balances comfortably on your spine
- Gently lift your shoulders squarely with your body
- Take several slow deep breaths to loosen your chest muscles
- Look up, look forward, look around.

Remember:

If you suppress your feelings, you depress your life.

Further Positives

Now adjust your mental attitude by catching those sentences causing the anxiety. Replace them with positive, strengthening and reinforcing thoughts or affirmations.

- "I can deal with these life experiences."
- "I am able to cope."
- "Life is okay and I am okay"
- "I can handle it." (The person, the situation, myself).

Feelings are part of being human so unblock these negative emotions. They are normal and natural feelings. There is no such thing as a negative emotion as all are valid, **it is how you handle them** which creates either negative or positive responses.

Enlightenment

Now put the mind and body connection into the enlightenment mode by valuing, appreciating and acknowledging. We can do this by:

- Watching a beautiful sunset
- Appreciating an exquisite rose
- Playing with children
- Soaking in warm relaxing baths
- Enjoying aromas - coffee, rain, natural scents
- Stroking your pets
- Listening to lively music
- Stimulating new ideas by reading
- Warming connections with friends
- Sensual feelings of soft silken materials
- Giving yourself treats
- Invigorating yourself with sports
- Waking with enthusiasm
- Absorbing the suns warmth
- Relaxing to soft, soothing music
- Completing a pleasurable task
- Listening to your heart

Enlightenment

- Luxuriating in bed
- Being invigorated by cool water
- Being absorbed in colours
- Quietening to the sounds of silence
- Making a connection with a stranger
- Laughing, giggling and having fun
- Surrounding yourself with joy - joyful sights, joyful sounds and joyful feelings.

Each of these strategies is designed to encourage relaxation and less of the 'stress boulder' we carry that depresses us in every area of ourselves and our lives. We are trying to 'lighten up' and have more meaningful attitudes.

Note:

Attitude is all for enlightenment, so...

- **straighten up,**
- **look up,**
- **think up,**
- **lighten up!**

Thought Stopping

When thoughts are distressing, a quick technique called 'Thought Stopping' can be used with several different methods.

One:
- Say the word **'Stop'** either in your mind or aloud.
- Repeat the word over and over again.
- Sing it, spell it out **S-T-O-P**, scream it, whisper it or chant it.
- Keep it going as long as you can.
- When the anxious thought returns, repeat the **'Stop'** as often as necessary.

Two:
- Picture a **Stop** sign in your mind.
- See the sharp angles of the sign.
- See the bright red centre colour.
- See the luminous white letter of the word **'Stop'**.
- Focus on this sign for as long as you can.

Thought Stopping

Three:
- Make the **Stop** sign a flashing neon light.
- Walk down a path and see a **Stop** sign at every step.
- Imagine driving a car along a street with a **Stop** sign at every corner.
- Picture a row of boxes and every time you take a lid off a **Stop** sign pops up from the box.
- Use your imagination to bring up **Stop** signs in your mind.

Repeat these images as long and as often as is necessary when the distressing thought re-occurs.

Another method of 'Thought Stopping' is the 'fixed gaze or staring' method, focusing on an object or subject. By focusing with complete concentration you are blocking out the worrying thoughts, thus allowing your stress level to reduce.

Contemplation of:

- a candle flame
- a beautiful flower
- a restful natural scene
- an exquisite crystal

will achieve this state, which is also called 'open eyed meditation'.

Thought Stopping

The I Ching Hexagram 61 is called 'Understanding' and it is a wonderful subject to focus upon. Put your gaze into the centre of the Hexagram and let go of your negative thoughts.

By copying this Hexagram on a larger sheet of paper in either red or black and placing it on a wall or door and occasionally focusing on this during the day for a period of three to five minutes, you will allow your mind to relax almost instantly.

Note:

As distressing thoughts are persistent, remember to be just as persistent with your stress reducing strategies, thus continually strengthening your mind both positively and constructively.

Relaxation

Stress reducing techniques can be used anywhere and under any circumstances.

Relaxation is the foundation for stress reducing techniques. If the relaxation response is not in place, any other coping mechanisms will only be partly effective, as the pressured mind and the tense body will need to be relaxed beforehand. By reducing these barriers, strategies will be more easily adopted, will work faster and, therefore, less energy is required.

Many people have excuses for not practicing relaxation techniques...

- I haven't got the time
- I haven't got a comfortable spot
- I haven't got the right oils
- I haven't got any soft music
- I haven't got the opportunity to be alone
- I haven't got the person to teach me.

In itself, lack of time is a prominent reason for stress related illness. Finding time and taking on **another task** can stop many people from trying relaxation techniques, but there are several levels of relaxation.

Relaxation

Fear can immobilise and trap us if we let it.

The perception of relaxation can also cause a fearful reaction. The reality is that relaxation gets a person back to a higher state of efficiency where physical and mental areas are able to become balanced.

Benefits are:

- Easier breathing
- Healthier body
- Consistent sleep patterns
- Better physical co-ordination
- Clearer mind
- Positive mental outlook
- Open emotional responses.

Most people have a favourite method of relaxing: walking, exercising, reading or listening to music. But true relaxation

Relaxation

is quietening the body and calming the mind. As the mind and body are connected, and therefore, always affecting each other, using a **physical technique** will calm the mind. By using a **mental technique** it will also still the body.

Developing the habit of practicing relaxation techniques without the need to think about them is a most important ability.

There are greater long-term benefits from the relaxation techniques of meditation, and it is recommended you take the opportunity to try this style of relaxation.

However, in practical terms the more **'spot' relaxations** you do through the day, the better you are at coping and dealing effectively with your stressors, as:

- You are dealing with the stress at the time it is occurring
- You are taking control of your situation
- You are gaining the benefit of the relaxation immediately
- You are not postponing it until you have the time, place and opportunity.

Note:

Oils, music and a special place are bonuses, but they are not essential, as the main requirement is a willingness to do the relaxation to assist the body and mind to reduce stress and tension.

Relaxation Techniques

Following are techniques which will range from two minutes to ten minutes in duration.

Ten Preparation Steps:

1. Seat yourself upright in a chair
2. Have your spine straight
3. Uncross your arms and legs
4. Gently move your head from side to side
5. Take in a normal breath
6. Let the breath out and close your eyes
7. Breathe in through the nose as you count to 4
8. Hold your breath to the count of 4
9. Breathe out through the mouth to the count of 4
10. Repeat three more times breathing in 4, hold 4 and out 4.

Relax whenever and wherever necessary.

Note:

These steps are to be used to prepare for either the physical or mental relaxation techniques.

Physical Relaxation

Time: 8 to 10 minutes

One

- Screw up toes
- Tighten instep
- Tighten muscles from ankle to knee
- Tighten muscles from knee to hip

Hold a slow count of 10

- Release upper leg muscles
- Release lower leg muscles
- Stretch feet and toes and rest them flat on the floor
- Let warmth flow down from the hips, through the legs to the toes

and relax...

Two

- Tighten the stomach muscles
- Clench cheeks of the buttocks tightly together
- Push lower part of the body into the seat

Hold to a slow count of 10

- Let the body lighten from the seat
- Let the buttocks soften
- Release the stomach muscles
- Let warmth flow down from the waist through the lower part of the body down through the legs to the toes

and relax...

Physical Relaxation

Three

- Take a slow, deep breath and expand the chest
- Continue to take in short breaths until the lungs are full
- Feel the tightness of the chest and back muscles

Hold as long as you can

In a controlled manner, part lips and allow breath to slowly release

- Then gently puff out the last remaining air
  and breathe softly
- Let warmth flow around the upper part of the body
  down the lower part of the body
  down through the legs to the toes

and relax...

Four

- Clench fingers one by one into the palm to form a tight fist
- Tighten arm muscles from wrist to elbow
- Tighten muscles from elbow to shoulder
- Pull arms in tightly to the body

Hold to a slow count of 10

- Allow shoulders to drop down
- Release upper arm muscles
- Release lower arm muscles
- Stretch fingers out one by one
- Rest arms and hands comfortably in your lap
- Let warmth flow down from shoulders to fingers
  through the upper part of the body
  and through the lower part of the body,
  then down the legs to the toes

and relax...

Physical Relaxation

Five

- Feel the tightness of your scalp stretching from ear to ear
- Clench your teeth together
- Press your tongue against the back of the teeth
- Squash your cheeks upwards
- Screw eyes tightly together
- Wrinkle up the forehead
- Push out the tendons in the neck

Hold to a slow count of 10

- Allow the tendons of the neck to soften
- Allow the teeth to come apart
- Let the jaw sag slightly
- Let the tongue rest comfortably in the mouth
- Feel cheeks sagging
- Lift eyebrows to release eye tightness
- Drop eyebrows to release forehead muscles
- Feel the tight band of scalp muscles soften
- Let warmth flow down the head
  down the face, neck and shoulders
  down the arms to the fingers
  down the upper part of the body
  down the lower part of the body
  down the legs to the toes

and relax...

Six

- Take in a breath and direct it to the top of the head
- Imagine there is a small hole in the head
- Now let the breath come out of this opening
- As the breath comes out it becomes gentle waves that wash down the outside of the body
- Warm rhythmic waves that wash away any remaining surface tension.
- Let warmth flow down the head, the face, neck and shoulders
- Down the arms to the fingers
- Down the upper part of the body
- Down the lower part of the body
- Down the legs to the toes and just wash away into the earth.

and relax...

The whole of your body is totally **relaxed**, **warm** and **comfortable**.

- When you are ready take a slow deep breath
- Become aware of your clothing and the chair you are seated in
- Take another deep breath being aware of how alert and bright you feel
- And with your third breath just open your eyes as you let your breath out.

Physical Relaxation

- You can work through these six steps for a complete body relaxation.
- You can choose just one step, e.g. head and neck if experiencing tightness or strain or headache, or the legs and feet if you have been sitting for a long period of time.
- You can have someone read these steps to you and follow through with them.
- You can tape these steps onto a cassette and play it to yourself.
- You can use this technique to go to sleep by changing the first preparation instruction to "Lay yourself down in a comfortable bed" and then listen to the cassette.

Mental Relaxation

Time: 5 - 7 minutes

- Work through the ten preparation steps.
- Count to three, and on the third count I want you to imagine you are standing at the beach, in a quiet secluded area where there are no other people.
- You can feel the warm dry sand under your bare feet. As you squeeze your toes together, you feel the dry gritty sand rubbing on the soles of your feet.
- You are facing the water and notice the clear blue of the sky, the line of the horizon as it meets the sea, and the rippling effect of the waves.
- You experience the warmth of the soft sun, as it melts like liquid honey all over your body.
- A gentle breeze slides past your skin like soothing fingers over your face.
- The salty tang of the sea water smells very refreshing.
- You are able to hear the relaxing sound of the waves lapping ahead of you.
- Everything about this scene makes you feel **warm**, **relaxed** and **comfortable**.
- You can feel the tension leaving your body, the tightness draining away, and peace, calmness and tranquillity filling your body from the toes to the crown of the head.
- You may choose to walk around in this scene, lay down on the sand and relax even more, or just stand still and let the feeling of bliss be experienced.

Mental Relaxation

- When you are ready take a slow deep breath and let the scene fade.
- Take another deep breath and be aware of how alert and bright you feel.
- And with your third breath just open your eyes and let your breath out.

Imagine you are standing on a secluded beach

Note

- You can use this technique for relaxing completely in preparation for sleep.

- You can change this scene from the beach to a garden, rainforest, waterfall area, or any natural outdoor area for which you may have an affinity.

Mental Relaxation

Time: 2 minutes

- Work through the ten preparation steps.
- Count to three and on the third count see before you a large door.
- This door is made of wood with a very large shiny brass handle on one side.
- You take hold of the handle and turn it to open the door.
- Push the door open, step inside and close it behind you.
- Inside the room you see before you a pink cloud at floor level.
- Walk over to the cloud and feel it.
- It is very soft and bouncy but also strong and supporting.
- Turn around and sit on the cloud.

Imagine yourself relaxing on a pink cloud.

Mental Relaxation

- The softness envelopes you as though you are cushioned by a silken pillow.
- Now lay back into the cloud.
- The warmth of the pink seeps through into your tight body and you feel the knots of tension loosening.
- You may experience a soft and gentle rocking sensation which helps relaxation even more.
- Allow a feeling of warmth, comfort and total relaxation.
- When ready stand up, walk to the door, and, after turning the handle, step outside the room closing the door behind you.
- You may come back to this room at any time.
- When ready take a slow deep breath and become aware of the room you are in.
- Take another deep breath and notice how alert and refreshed you feel.
- With a third breath open your eyes as you slowly release the breath.

Note:

This is a quick technique which can be used at work when you feel uptight or a social scene when you feel your anxiety level rising.

Perhaps when driving there may be occasions when pulling over to the kerb is a sensible move. For your safety, as well as others, it is obvious driving should occur with a relaxed state of mind.

Time Out

'Time out' is called in sports when the players need to rest, catch their breath, and re-focus on the game plan.

It is appropriate to call a 'time out' during stressful stages in life.

'Time out' may only need to be a short period (5 minutes or more) or it may need to be much longer depending on your degree of anxiety.

5 minutes	Walk outside
10 minutes	Listen to music
15 minutes	Enjoy a cup of tea, coffee, water, etc
20 minutes	Stroll around the block or through a garden
1 hour	Drive to the beach and look at the sea
2 hours	Go to a light hearted or escapist movie
5 hours	Spend the afternoon wandering through shops, parks, libraries, galleries, etc
24 hours	Book into a bed and breakfast or hotel overnight.

Important

- Remember to leave your worries when you go.
- Use the time out to refresh your mind and body.
- Bring back positive benefits into your normal situation.
- Keep re-focusing on the positive feelings.

Self Massage

Massage is magic to relieving stress.

Regular sessions with a qualified therapist will work to relieve both the physical and mental strain experienced during stressful periods, releasing knotted muscles and aid in calming the thoughts.

There are also methods of self massage which can relieve tension quickly.

Simple objects such as stones and balls can be utilised for fast spot relaxations.

Massage One - Hands & Feet

Select a stone about the size of your palm with a smooth surface and a flat area on one side, and gentle curves on the other. You can purchase a stone in a crystal shop or find one in a creek bed or beach area.

Place the stone flat side down on a firm surface, put your hand over the stone and move your hand around gently pressing the high spots of the stone into your palm and fingers.

Press, **hold** and **move** working around the outside of the palm and down the length of each finger. Pressure should be firm enough to allow a feeling of warmth after the area is lifted from the curve, but not so hard that the muscles of the arm have to be used to push the hand down on to the stone.

This is a quick technique (1 to 2 minutes) and can be used at work to relax hands with computer cramp.

Placing the stone on the floor, remove your shoes and place your foot over the stone. Move your foot around gently pressing the heel, toes and instep against the curves of the stone.

Press, **hold** and **move** working around the outside of the shape of the foot as well. Do not use the leg muscles to push the foot down too firmly, use mainly foot pressure.

Another quick technique (1 to 2 minutes) to relieve tightness.

Massage Two - Face

Select a stone that is flat, round and very smooth which is comfortably held with the fingers.

When there is tightness and tension in the face or head area, put the massage stone on the forehead between the eyebrows and hold gently in place allowing the sensation of coolness to become the focus.

Then slide the stone over the skin around the eyebrow down to the side of the eye and **hold** with gentle pressure.

Slide the stone along the cheekbone to the side of the nose and **hold** with gentle pressure.

Slide the stone on to the top lip and **hold** with gentle pressure in the spot under the centre of the nose.

Gently circle the lips and slide the stone to the centre of the chin and **hold** with gentle pressure.

Then repeat all steps starting from the forehead to the chin for the opposite side of the face.

This is a simple technique (1 to 2 minutes), the movement, gentle pressure and coolness of the pebble will achieve positive results.

Massage Three - Back

Using a squash and golf ball.

To relieve tight back and shoulder muscles stand with your back to a wall.

Put the squash ball between your shoulder blades, and by rolling your body from side to side and bending your knees you can manipulate the ball along the upper shoulders and the shoulder blade area.

Use firm pressure but not uncomfortably so, as this movement is to relieve tight muscles, rather than have them tense with pain and discomfort.

Now place the squash ball in the middle of the back next to the spine, and manipulate the ball up and down the spinal column by bending and straightening the knees.

Do not have the ball just on the spine but also on the muscles adjacent the spine.

By moving the body side to side you can manipulate the ball in a zigzag movement across the spine.

After you have worked on this area and can feel some warmth, remove the squash ball and replace it with the golf ball. Then repeat the same movements.

Massage Three

Caution:

Again, if it is uncomfortable then do not go on.

If you find this is too sensitive do not continue using the golf ball at this time.

Do not run the golf ball over the spinal column.

Lower back and hips.

Using the squash ball, manipulate this area of the lower back and hips using the rolling body movement and knee bends. As this area is generally bone structure, the golf ball needs to be used with very light pressure.

Feet, hands and even the lower part of the arms can be relaxed using either ball. Simply place the ball on a firm surface and gently apply pressure while rolling between the skin and the firm surface.

Note:

To be healthy, energy needs to **flow** smoothly through our body.

- Tightness causes **Barriers** to the flow.
- Massage allows **Movement** of the flow.

Aromatherapy

The use of leaves, flowers and herbs to promote good health has been documented for thousand of years.

The most common techniques used are baths, massages, teas, food, inhalation and skin application.

Aromatherapy uses essential oils to **restore** the balance, **revive** the emotions and **heal** the body.

Caution:

Do **not** take essential oils internally.

- Massage
  - stimulating
  - calming
- Baths and inhalants
  - rejuvenate
  - relax
  - restore
- Teas, herbs
  - enjoyment
  - enhancement
  - digestion
  - detoxify
  - improve health
- Skin applications
  - treatments
  - beautify

Aromatherapy Baths

It is wise to purchase essential oils. Although more expensive, they are pure and will provide the most beneficial results.

Cheaper synthetic aromatics do not have the same effect on the body and nervous system and in burners the synthetics can even cause allergic reactions.

Baths: A soothing bath will refresh you completely and is a wonderful way of restoring and rejuvenating yourself before going out. Also before bedtime allowing you to drift easily into sleep.

Do not have the bath too hot - it drains energy, and is not relaxing. The temperature should feel warmer than your hand, but not make your skin colour with the heat.

Brew Mix

Make strong brew in a pot with herbs in boiling water then pour the liquid into the bath.

Mix - 8 bags of camomile

Herb Steep

Place herbs in cloth bag (stocking wash bags are great for this).

Aromatherapy

Start the bath with just hot water leaving the herb bag to soak. Then remove the bag and run the bath to a comfortable temperature. You may leave the bag in if you wish.

Herb Mix:

A cup of **lavender**

Or a cup of camomile

Or a cup of lavender and one of rose

Or a cup of camomile and one of rose

Oil Soak

Run the bath at a comfortable temperature and then pour the oils into the water.

Oil blend:

4 drops of lavender and 3 of geranium

Or 4 drops of rosemary and 3 of sage

Or 4 drops of rosemary and 3 of geranium

Or 4 drops of rose and 3 of lavender

Note:

Candles and soft, soothing music will enhance the relaxation and pleasure of this bath-time treat.

Aromatherapy Vapourisers

Essential oils when used in oil burners will assist a calming effect with improved mental clarity and elevating your mood. Burners can be used in an office or home to create an appropriate atmosphere.

Fill the water bowl, light the burner and use any one of the combinations below.

Relaxation:

Lavender . . . . .3 drops

Rose . . . . .3 drops

Mental Clarity:

Rosemary . . . . .2 drops

Lemon . . . . .2 drops

Eucalyptus . . . . .2 drops

Invigoration:

Lemongrass . . . . .2 drops

Sage . . . . .2 drops

Pine . . . . .2 drops

Inspiration:

Basil . . . . .2 drops

Bergamot . . . . .2 drops

Stress Styles

Most people tend to think of stress as,

Overwork = overload = burnout

But there is another style of stress which is equally as destructive to a positive, happy life.

This is the stress of,

Underwork = boredom = rustout

and these styles are on opposite ends of the stress scale.

Rustout stress can be caused by:

- being confined - illness, home duties
- doing a repetitive job
- lack of social contact - at home, unemployed
- unchanging lifestyle - work, T.V., cook, clean, sleep.

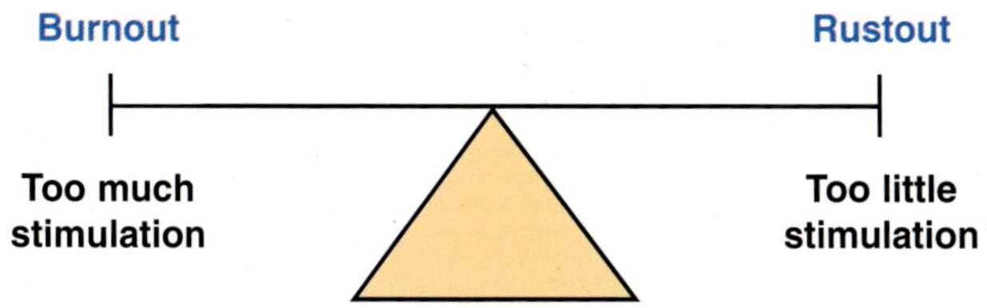

Both burnout and rustout produce distress to the mind and body resulting in both mental and physical symptoms.

The stress symptoms range from:

- Disturbed sleep - to - overlong sleep
- No appetite - to - always hungry
- Explosive behaviours - to - no responses
- Loose bowels - to - constipation
- Hyperactive - to - lethargic
- Supersensitive - to - feeling numb.

Note:

Any of these responses are warning signals to take notice and **take notice now**.

Balance

The main way to deal with either stress style is **balance**.

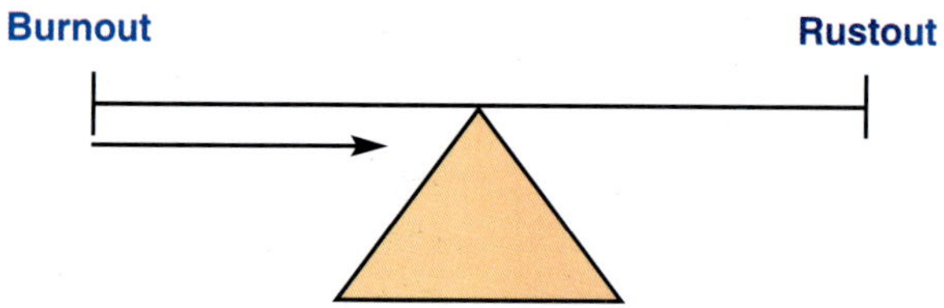

How can you move from burnout to balance?

Overstimulation:

- Mentally can lead to brain fatigue
- Physically, to health problems
- Socially, to total exhaustion.

So the mind, body and self need to **relax**.

Quieten your mind by:

- listening to soft music
- sitting in a park.

Restore the body by:

- gentle massage
- sitting still, laying down
- aromatherapy baths / showers.

Revive the self by:

- appreciating beauty
- quiet positive activities
- creating a relaxed atmosphere.

Balance

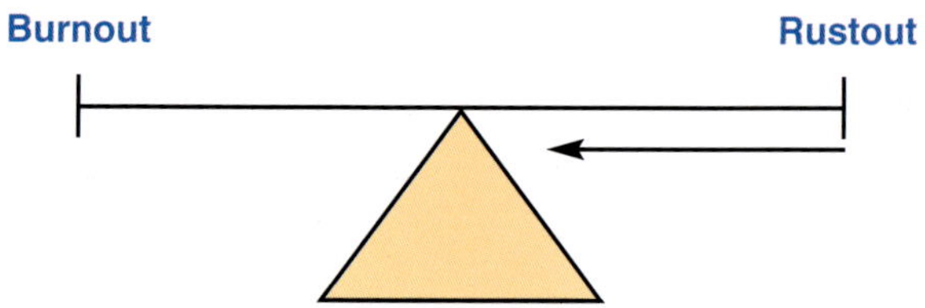

How can you move from rustout to balance?

Understimulation:

- Mentally can lead to dull thinking
- Physically to health problems
- Socially to a lonely life through low self esteem.

So the mind, body and self need to **workout**.

Stimulate your mind by:

- reading positive books
- studying an interesting subject
- enjoying humourous articles.

Work your body by:

- a vigorous walk around the block - twice
- dancing to fast music
- energetic window washing.

Activate your sense of self by:

- ringing a friend for a positive chat
- attending a class on any subject you enjoy
- start a conversation as often as you can with people you don't already know.

Balance

Therefore, the single most important factor to deal with stress is...

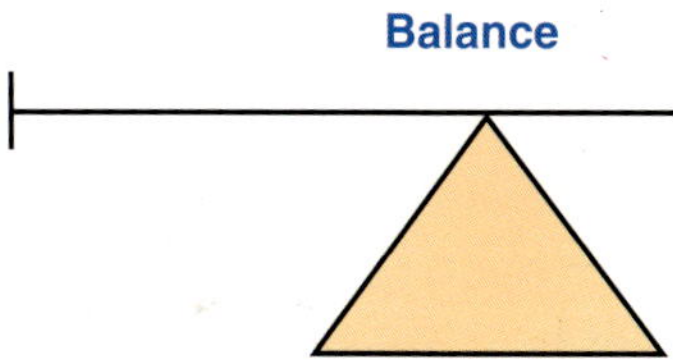

Always look for ways to get balance into your life whether at work, home, socially or by yourself.

It is most important to remember **and continue emphasising to yourself** that life is not predictable and you will experience highs and lows, both great and small, in both positive and negative experiences.

As life's fluctuations are perfectly natural, it is important to realise your response in attitude and action is what determines your perceptions and ultimate balance.

So when you get knocked off balance - re-balance.

Note:

Balance is the key to a positive, happy and constructive life.

Take Control

Use these steps to control your stress.

Be Aware!

Know your personal stress signs - physical, mental or emotional and be concerned if they start to occur frequently. This may well be a warning sign for you to make adjustments.

Take Steps

Have strategies in place to reduce the cause and the effect of the stress.

Do It

Whether they are continual stress reducing techniques, e.g meditation, yoga exercise program, etc. or quick spot tension relievers, e.g. music, aromatherapy, etc. The secret is,

to do it!

Knowing

what to do is important but

Doing

it is the only way to:

- make changes
- improve your life
- feel empowered and...

Be yourself

as you truly want to be.

The Journey of a Thousand Miles Begins with a First Step...

the First Steps series

- First Steps to Meditation
- First Steps to Massage
- First Steps to Chi Kung
- First Steps to Tarot
- First Steps to Dream Power
- First Steps to Yoga
- First Steps to Palmistry
- First Steps to Feng Shui
- First Steps to Managing Stress
- First Steps to Astrology
- First Steps to Numerology
- First Steps to Acupressure

Further titles following shortly

•AXIOM DISTRIBUTORS Pty Ltd.
Unit 2, 1 Union Street, Stepney, South Australia, 5069